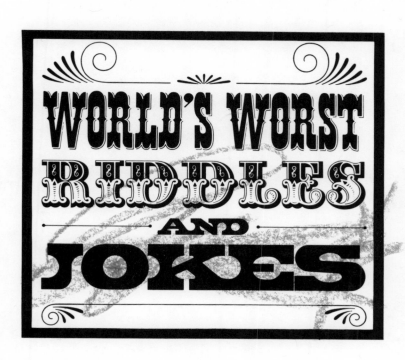

WORLD'S WORST RIDDLES AND JOKES

WORLD'S WORST
RIDDLES
AND
JOKES

BY BILL ADLER

ILLUSTRATED BY ED MALSBERG

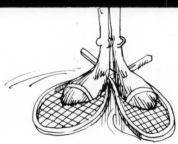

GROSSET & DUNLAP
A FILMWAYS COMPANY
Publishers • New York

Library of Congress Catalog Card Number: 76-6819
ISBN: 0-448-12586-2 (Trade Edition)
ISBN: 0-448-13382-2 (Library Edition)

1978 PRINTING

CONTENTS

	Page
The Animal Kingdom	8
Birds and Insects	18
Fish	21
Weird and Ghostly	24
Pickle Jokes	27
Elephant Jokes	29
Knock-Knock Jokes	32
Moron Jokes	38
Very Little Sense	40
One-Liners	48
Wit Around the World	52
Occupations	58
Business Before Pleasure	66
School Days	70
Moms and Dads	77
Dining Out	80
Good for What Ails You	85
Limericks	92
Riddle Me This	95

THE ANIMAL KINGDOM

Doctor: What's the trouble?
Kangaroo: I haven't been feeling jumpy lately.

Why is a rabbit's nose always shiny?
Because his powder puff is on the wrong end.

When is a horse never hungry?
When it has a bit in its mouth.

What's another name for a smart duck?
A wise quacker.

Question: What kind of corsage did Lassie wear to the ball?
Answer: A collie flower.

A hippopotamus is sitting on a chair. What time is it?
Time to get a new chair.

Why does a polar bear wear a fur coat?
Because he'd look funny in a woolen one.

What do you call an animal who is ten feet tall, has five arms, and poisonous fingernails?
"Sir."

Father Kangaroo: Where's the baby?
Mother Kangaroo: Oh, no! I've had my pocket picked!

8

What do you give a seasick lion?
Lots of room!

How do you keep a skunk from smelling?
You hold his nose.

What is a tiger called who ate its father's sister?
An aunt-eater.

"I wish I had enough money to buy a hippopotamus."
"A hippopotamus? What do you want a hippopotamus for?"
"I don't. I just want the money."

How can you make a tortoise fast?
Take his food away.

Why do baby pigs eat so much?
They all want to make hogs of themselves.

What squeals more loudly than a pig caught under a fence?
Two pigs.

If one pig is in a pen and another pig is running loose in the farmyard, which one is singing, "Don't fence me in"?
Neither one—pigs can't sing.

He: "What's the difference between a sigh, a car, and a donkey?"
She: "I give up."
He: "Well, a sigh is 'Oh, dear!' A car is too dear."
She: "And what's a donkey?"
He: "You, dear."

Adam and Eve were naming the animals of the earth, when along came a rhinoceros.
Adam said, "What shall we call this one?"
"Let's call it a rhinoceros," suggested Eve.
"Why?" asked Adam.
"Well," said Eve, "it looks more like a rhinoceros than anything else we've seen."

Why does a giraffe eat so little?
Because a little goes a long way.

What has the head of a cat, the tail of a cat, and is not a cat?
A kitten.

What's the principal part of a horse?
The mane part.

What is black and white, and has sixteen wheels?
A zebra on roller skates.

What has four legs and flies?
A dead horse.

What do you get when you cross a cow and a pogo stick?
A milkshake.

What did the beaver say to the tree?
"It's been nice gnawing you."

What did the monkey say as he laid his tail on the railroad tracks?
"It won't be long now."

What farm animal is a cannibal?
A cow. It eats its fodder.

What is the hardest key to turn?
A donkey.

When will a cat usually enter a house?
When the door is open.

What two animals go with you everywhere you go, all the time?
Your calves.

What is worse than raining cats and dogs?
Hailing taxis.

What does every crocodile become when it first takes to the water?
Wet.

What does a 500-pound mouse say to a cat?
"Here, kitty, kitty, kitty!"

10

How do you look at a hippo's teeth?
Very carefully!

What would you call a sleeping bull?
A bulldozer.

What kind of keys won't open a door?
Monkeys, turkeys, and donkeys.

What do giraffes have that no other animal has?
Baby giraffes.

What is the weakest animal in the world?
A frog: he will croak if you touch him.

Who always goes to sleep wearing his shoes?
A horse.

What does a lion become after it is one year old?
Two years old.

Why is a cat longer at night than in the morning?
Because he is taken in in the morning, and let out at night.

What is black and white and red all over?
A blushing zebra.

What's the worst weather for rats and mice?

When it's raining cats and dogs.

Two sheep were in the country. The first sheep said, "Baaa." The second sheep said, "Moo." Again, the first sheep said, "Baaa." The second sheep said, "Moo."

"Sheep don't say Moo," said the first sheep.

"I know," replied the second sheep. "I'm practicing a foreign language."

"We can't keep horses in our house. Imagine the smell."

"Why worry? They'll get used to it."

He: "If you were surrounded by twenty lions, fifteen tigers, and ten leopards, how would you get away from them?"

She: "Stop the merry-go-round and get off!"

Question: What do you call a monkey that sells potato chips?

Answer: A chip monk.

He: "What kind of dog is that?"
She: "He's a police dog."
He: "He sure doesn't look like one to me."
She: "Of course not. He's in the Secret Service."

What animal would be likely to eat a relative?
An ant-eater.

A cat in despondency sighed
And resolved to commit suicide.
    She passed under the wheels
    Of eight automobiles,
And after the ninth one she died.

What does a horse say to oats?
"Neigh!"

First Dog: "My name is Fido. What's yours?"
Second Dog: "I'm not sure, but I think it's Down Boy."

"So you like my dog," said Alice. "I'm glad. It's a very rare breed. Part boxer and part bull. It cost me a thousand dollars."
"Really?" said Sandra. "Which part is the bull?"
"The part about the thousand dollars."

Why doesn't Sweden send to other countries for cattle?
Because she keeps a good Stock-holm.

What is the best way to catch a squirrel?
Go climb a tree and make a noise like a nut.

Why is ice cream like a race horse?
The more you lick it, the faster it goes.

Guide on Safari: "Now, remember what I told you—when you see that leopard, shoot him on the spot."
Gamehunter: "Which spot?"

Two skunks, born gamblers, played cards for a scent a point.

A cow, under analysis, claimed she had a fodder complex.

When the lion-hunter failed to return to camp, one of his fellow hunters shook his head and said, "He must have disagreed with something that ate him."

What could a lion eat after it had its teeth pulled?
Its dentist.

What is a lion called who eats its mother and father?
An orphan.

Do lions have good memories?
Yes, they never forget elephant jokes!

Why did the lion wear red suspenders?
The blue ones broke!

What's the toughest job for a lion?
Trying to find a dentist who'll see him twice a year!

What do you call a lion hunter who uses a peashooter?
Stupid!

What would you call a man who sticks his hand into a lion's mouth?
Lefty!

What do lions have that no other animals have?
Baby lions!

What's more unusual than a talking dog?
A spelling bee.

If twenty dogs run after one dog, what time is it?
Twenty after one.

Sally: "See that dog chasing his tail."
Paul: "Poor little cuss! He's trying to make both ends meet."

What dog keeps the best time?
A watch dog.

A duck, a frog and a skunk went to the circus. Tickets were a dollar. Who got in, and who didn't?
The duck got in because she had a bill.
The frog got in on his greenback.
But the poor old skunk couldn't get in because he had only a scent, and it was a bad one at that.

A mink said to her litter. "The last shall be furs."

A shepherd, when asked why he kept giving aspirin to his sheep, replied, "It's just a question of baa relief."

Where were the dogs and cats when the lights went out?
In the dark.

What do you get when you cross a cactus and a porcupine?
You get sore hands.

What tree is like a pet?
Dogwood.

Why is it hard for a leopard to hide in the jungle?
'Cause he's always spotted.

What is brown, has a hump, and lives at the North Pole?
Rudolph the Red-Nosed Camel.

16

"Would you believe it—my dog doesn't even have a nose!"
"Then how does he smell?"
"Terrible."

"My dog, Rex, doesn't have a tail."
"Then how can you tell when he's happy?"
"He stops biting me."

Customer: "I thought you said this dog was a good watchdog."
Pet Shop Owner: "Well, isn't he?"
Customer: "Certainly not. Last night he barked so loudly that the burglars came and went without our hearing them."

A dog is man's best friend, but nobody has told that to a police dog.

Once a hunter in the woods lost his dog, so he put his ear next to a tree and listened to the bark.

Why does a dog wag his tail? Because no one else will wag it for him.

Guest: "Why does your dog sit there and watch me eat?"
Host: "I can't imagine, unless it's because you have the plate he usually eats from."

BIRDS AND INSECTS

Why do birds fly south for the winter?
Because it's too far to walk.

Why does a stork stand on one leg?
So it won't fall over.

If a chicken could talk, what kind of
language would it speak?
Foul language.

What bird can you find in Canada,
and though it has wings, can't fly?
A dead one.

Boy: "Why did the chicken cross the
road?"
Girl: "For fowl reasons."

Why did the chicken cross the road?
To get away from Colonel Sanders.

"Did you hear the story about the
peacock?"
"Nope."
"It's a beautiful tale."

What do birds say on Halloween?
"Trick or tweet."

A man bought an expensive talking bird at a pet shop to surprise his wife. She wasn't home when he arrived; so he left the bird for her and went to work.

When he returned home for dinner that evening, he discovered that his wife had cooked the bird for supper.

"Why did you do it?" the man exclaimed. "That was a rare talking bird. It cost one hundred dollars."

"How was I to know?" the wife replied. "He didn't say anything to me!"

What does a duck have that no other bird has?
Ducklings.

Why is a rooster a very particular bird?
He won't lend anyone his comb.

First Pelican: "Pretty good fish you have there."
Second Pelican: "Well, it fills the bill."

Little Boy: "I would like a quarter's worth of bird seed, please."
Saleslady: "How many birds do you have, dear?"
Little Boy: "None, but I want to grow some."

What ants are the largest?
Giants.

What is smaller than an insect's mouth?
What the insect eats.

What is a Boobee?
It's a little bug that hides in flowers and scares bees.

Should you ever eat chicken on an empty stomach?
No—always use a plate!

What do you get when you cross a chicken and a bell?
You get an alarm cluck.

When the little chicken found an orange in his mother's straw box, the little chicken said, "Look at the orange marmalade."

Boy: "Do insects have brains?"
Girl: "Of course, insects have brains. How else could they figure out when you're going to have a picnic?"

Question: Who was the first skin-diver?
Answer: A mosquito.

Why does a spider make a good baseball player?
Because he catches flies.

Why do bumblebees hum?
Because they don't know the words.

What was the worm doing in the cornfield?
Going in one ear and out the other.

Mike: "Did you know that a grass-hopper can jump a distance that is fifty times its own length?"
Ted: "No, but I've seen a wasp lift a 250-pound man three feet off the ground."

FISH

A fisherman was having a wonderful time in a trout stream. Of course, the fishing season hadn't opened and he didn't have a license, but he was having a wonderful time, anyhow.

Finally, a stranger walked up.

"Any luck?" asked the stranger.

"Any luck! Boy, oh, boy! This is a wonderful spot. I took forty fish out of this stream yesterday."

"Is that so? By the way," the stranger said, "do you know who I am?"

"Nope."

"Well, meet the game warden," said the stranger.

"Oh," gulped the fisherman. "Well, do you know who I am?"

"Nope."

"Well, meet the biggest liar in the state."

How can you tell a shark owner in a pet shop?
He's the one buying a two-mile leash!

What do you think the shark did when he first met the octopus?
He shook its hand, hand, hand, hand, hand, hand, hand, hand!

Why did the whale cross the road?
To get to the other tide!

What is the best shark-repellent known to man?
The Sahara Desert!

What do you think really happened when Charlie the tuna swam away from the shark?
He became chicken of the sea!

Why do most fish hate gangsters?
Because they always carry a rod!

What made the tuna blush?
It saw the salad dressing.

What did one goldfish say to the other as they swam in the bowl?
"See you around."

What goes clomp, clomp, clomp, clomp, clomp, clomp, clomp, squoosh?
An octopus with one shoe off.

Why didn't the whale want to stay home at night?
Because it was married to a crab!

Why do fish hate tennis?
They don't want to get too close to the net!

What are the two words that will always make a shark happy?
"Man overboard!"

He: "I saw a man-eating shark at the aquarium."
She: "That's nothing. I saw a man eating herring in the restaurant."

Why are fish so smart?
Because they travel in schools.

Where does a jellyfish get its jelly?
From ocean currents.

Why do fish hate Coca-Cola?
Because it's the reel thing!

Boy: "I have a feeling my goldfish is very intelligent. How can I communicate with him?"
Girl: "Drop him a line."

Mother: "Susie, did you wash the fish before baking it?"
Susie: "No, Mom. Why should I wash a fish that's lived all its life in water?"

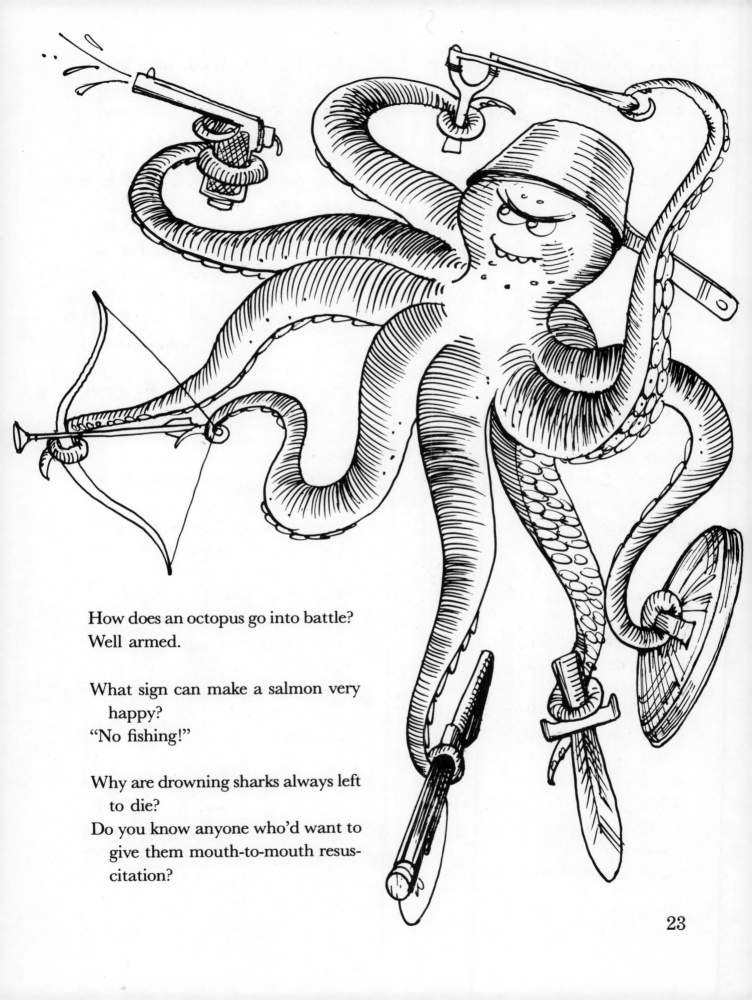

How does an octopus go into battle?
Well armed.

What sign can make a salmon very
    happy?
"No fishing!"

Why are drowning sharks always left
    to die?
Do you know anyone who'd want to
    give them mouth-to-mouth resus-
    citation?

WEIRD AND GHOSTLY

What did the vampire's son do on
the baseball team?
He was the batboy.

What do skeletons do when they lose
a hand?
They go to a second-hand store.

Where does a vampire plant flowers?
In a bat-tanical garden.

Where does a witch keep her space-
ship?
In the broom closet.

What was the vampire doing driving on the turnpike?
Looking for the main artery!

What happens in a vampire horse
race?
They finish neck and neck.

What advice did the father vampire
give his teen-age son?
Always bite the hand that feeds you!

What happens when vampires get
together?
They drive each other bats!

What does a skeleton do when it
   loses its head?
It calls a head hunter.

What is the best time to tell scary
   stories?
When the spirits move you.

What did the mother ghost say to
   the baby ghost?
"Fasten your sheet belt."

How do vampires travel?
By blood vessel.

What happened when the girl skeleton met the boy skeleton?
It was love at first fright.

What is a skeleton?
Some bones with the people scraped
   off.

Where do vampires keep their pre-
   cious possessions?
In a blood bank.

Why is there always a fence around
   a cemetery?
Because so many people are dying to
   get in.

What composer do vampires like
   best?
Bat-hoven.

What sort of music do mummies like
   best?
Ragtime.

Where do skeletons get their mail?
At the dead-letter office.

How does a witch tell time?
With her witch watch.

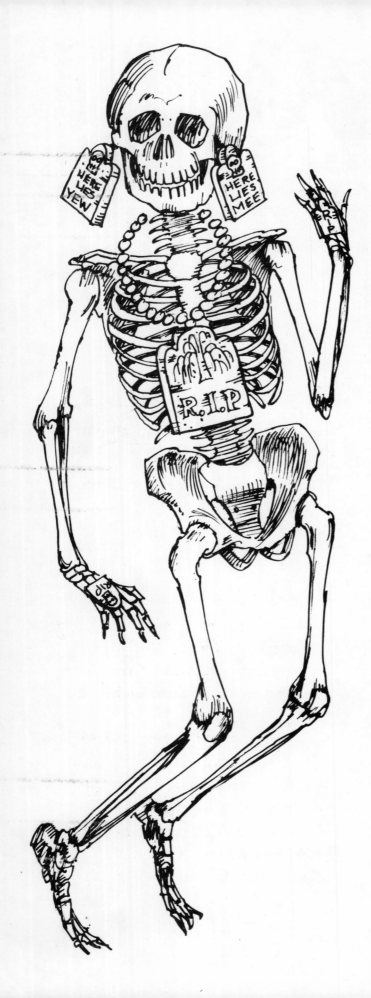

What kind of jewels does a skeleton wear?
Tombstones.

What did the vampire do when the panhandler stopped him and said he hadn't had a bite in days?
He bit him!

What do ghosts eat for breakfast?
Ghost Toasties and evaporated milk.

What do ghosts eat for lunch?
Boo-loney sandwiches.

What does a werewolf eat for a snack?
Ladyfingers.

What do ghosts wear on their feet in the rain?
Ghoul-oshes.

Who won the monster beauty contest?
Nobody.

Why are ghosts like the driving rain?
Because they are always in sheets.

What do monsters do to stop from dying?
They go into the living room.

What ballet do monsters like best?
"Swamp Lake."

PICKLE JOKES

How do you pack 1,000 pickles into a small barrel?
Very carefully!

What happens when a pickle is bored?
He becomes very dill.

How can you change a pickle into another vegetable?
You toss it in the air and it comes down squash!

Man: "Miss Smith, why is there a pickle behind your ear?"
Miss Smith: "Oh, dear, I must have eaten my pencil for lunch!"

What's green and green and green and green and green...
A pickle rolling downhill!

What do you call a dill that keeps changing color?
A fickle pickle!

What made the pickle break up with his fiance?
He soured on her.

How can you tell which pickles are left-handed?
Place a giant bowl of pickles in front of someone, ask him to eat as many as he can, and the remaining pickles are left!

When a cucumber tours England, where does it go first?
Pickledilly Circus.

"Hey, Billy, you've got a pickle in your ear."
"What'd you say?"
"I SAID, YOU'VE GOT——"
"You'll have to speak louder—I've got a pickle in my ear."

How do we know pickles are extremely jealous?
They turn green with envy!

What did one cucumber say to the other?
"Boy, are we going to be pickled!"

ELEPHANT JOKES

What is the difference between an elephant and a flea?

An elephant can have fleas, but a flea can't have elephants.

How does an elephant get down from a tree?

He climbs out on a leaf and waits for autumn.

How do you get down off an elephant?

You don't get down off an elephant; you get down off a duck.

Why does the elephant wear dark glasses?

If you had all those jokes told about you, you wouldn't want to be recognized, either.

Why do elephants have wrinkled ankles?

They lace their sneakers too tightly.

Why are elephants so wrinkled?

Did you ever try to iron one?

What did the grape say when the elephant stepped on it?

Nothing—it just let out a little whine.

What's gray on the inside and clear on the outside?

An elephant in a Baggie.

Why is an elephant gray, large, and wrinkled?

Because if he were small, white, and round, he would be an aspirin.

How can you tell when there is an elephant in your sandwich?
When it is too heavy to lift.

What can you say about nine elephants wearing pink sneakers and one elephant wearing blue?
Nine out of ten elephants wear pink sneakers.

What is the difference between an elephant and a jar of peanut butter?
The elephant doesn't stick to the roof of your mouth.

What words do you use to scold a bad elephant?
Tusk! Tusk!

An elephant never forgets. But what does an elephant have to remember, anyway?

Why did the elephant sit on the marshmallow?
So he wouldn't fall in the cocoa.

What luggage would you find in the jungle?
Elephant trunks.

Ted: "What's the difference between an elephant and a matterbaby?"

Alice: "What's a matterbaby?"

Ted: "Nothing, dear. What's the matter with you?"

How do you fit five elephants into a Volkswagen?

Two in the front, two in the back, and one in the glove compartment.

When is an elephant heavier than an elephant?.

When it's led.

How do you keep an elephant from charging?

Take away his credit card.

What do you call elephants who ride on airplanes?

Passengers.

What did Tarzan say when he saw the elephants coming?

"Here come the elephants."

Why aren't elephants allowed on the beach?

Because they can't keep their trunks up.

KNOCK-KNOCK JOKES

"Knock, knock!"
"Who's there?"
"Osborn."
"Osborn who?"
"Osborn in Tennessee."

"Knock, knock!"
"Who's there?"
"Otis."
"Otis who?"
"Otis room is a mess."

"Knock, knock!"
"Who's there?"
"Vera!"
"Vera who?"
"Vera interesting."

"Knock, knock!"
"Who's there?"
"Who!"
"Who who?"
"You make a good owl."

"Knock, knock!"
"Who's there?"
"Winnie!"
"Winnie who?"
"Winnie the Pooh, not who."

"Knock, knock!"
"Who's there?"
"Hutch."
"Hutch who?"
"Gesundheit!"

"Knock, knock!"
"Who's there?"
"Sarah."
"Sarah, who?"
"Sarah doctor in the house?"

"Knock, knock!"
"Who's there?"
"Elsie."
"Elsie who?"
"Elsie you later, alligator."

"Knock, knock!"
"Who's there?"
"Eileen."
"Eileen who?"
"Eileen on the fence and it broke."

"Knock, knock!"
"Who's there?"
"Alaska!"
"Alaska who?"
"Alaska a question and she'll give me an answer."

Betty: "Will you remember me in two years?"
Billy: "Yes."
Betty: "Will you remember me in four years?"
Billy: "Yes."
Betty: "Will you remember me in ten years?"
Billy: "Yes."
Betty: "Knock, knock!"
Billy: "Who's there?"
Betty: "See—you forgot me already!"

"Knock, knock!"
"Who's there?"
"Avon."
"Avon who?"
"Avon to be alone!"

"Knock, knock!"
"Who's there?"
"Boo."
"Boo who?"
"Don't cry, little baby."

"Knock, knock!"
"Who's there?"
"Dishes."
"Dishes who?"
"Dishes the FBI. Open up!"

"Knock, knock!"
"Who's there?"
"Accordion."
"Accordion who?"
"Accordion to the paper it's gonna
    snow tonight."

"Knock, knock!"
"Who's there?"
"Major."
"Major who?"
"Major open the door, didn't I?"

"Knock, knock!"
"Who's there?"
"Hugh."
"Hugh who?"
"Yoo hoo, yourself!"

"Knock, knock!"
"Who's there?"
"Butch and Jimmy!"
"Butch and Jimmy who?"
"Butch your arms around me and
    Jimmy a kiss."

"Knock, knock!"
"Who's there?"
"Doughnut."
"Doughnut who?"
"Doughnut ask me stupid ques-
    tions."

"Knock, knock!"
"Who's there?"
"Axle."
"Axle who?"
"Axle me no questions and I'll tell
    you no lies."

"Knock, knock!"
"Who's there?"
"Banana."
"Knock, knock!"
"Who's there?"
"Banana."
"Knock, knock!"
"Who's there?"
"Banana."
"Knock, knock!"
"Who's there?"
"Orange."
"Orange who?"
"Orange you glad I didn't say
    banana?"

"Knock, knock!"
"Who's there?"
"Mandy."
"Mandy who?"
"Mandy lifeboats!"

"Knock, knock!"
"Who's there?"
"Pickle."
"Pickle who?"
"Pickle letter from A to Z."

"Knock, knock!"
"Who's there?"
"Dwayne."
"Dwayne who?"
"Dwayne the bathtub! I'm dwowning!"

"Knock, knock!"
"Who's there?"
"The Avon lady. Your doorbell's broken."

"Knock, knock!"
"Who's there?"
"Jamaica."
"Jamaica who?"
"Jamaica passing grade in history?"

"Knock, knock!"
"Who's there?"
"Orange."
"Orange who?"
"Orange you ever going home?"

"Knock, knock!"
"Who's there?"
"Turnip."
"Turnip who?"
"Turnip the sound."

"Knock, knock!"
"Who's there?"
"Pizza."
"Pizza who?"
"Pizza on earth, good will to men."

"Knock, knock!"
"Who's there?"
"Thesis."
"Thesis who?"
"Thesis a recording."

"Knock, knock!"
"Who's there?"
"Leif."
"Leif who?"
"Leif me alone!"

"Knock, knock!"
"Who's there?"
"Arthur!"
"Arthur who?"
"Arthur mometer is broken."

"Knock, knock!"
"Who's there?"
"Zing."
"Zing who?"
"Zing a song of sixpence."

"Knock, knock!"
"Who's there?"
"Police!"
"Police who?"
"Police let me in."

"Knock, knock!"
"Who's there?"
"Hence!"
"Hence who?"
"Hence lay eggs."

"Knock, knock!"
"Who's there?"
"My panther!"
"My panther who?"
"My panther falling."

"Knock, knock!"
"Who's there?"
"Lettuce!"
"Lettuce who?"
"Lettuce in and you'll find out."

MORON JOKES

Why did the moron give cough
 syrup to the pony?
Someone told him it was a little
 horse.

First Moron: Did you just take a
 shower?
Second Moron: Why, is one miss-
 ing?

Why did the moron save burned-out
 light bulbs?
So he could use them in his dark-
 room.

Why did the moron ask his father to
 sit in the refrigerator?
He wanted ice-cold pop!

What did the moron say when they
 told him he was putting a saddle
 on backwards?
"How do you know which way I'm
 going?"

Why did the moron pitch a tent on
 top of the stove?
So he could have a home on the
 range.

Why did the moron want to be an
 electrician?
To get a charge out of life.

Why did the moron cut a hole in the
 rug?
So he could see the floor show.

Why did the moron go to night school?
So he could learn to read in the dark.

Why did the moron keep looking down all the time?
The doctor told him to watch his stomach.

Why did the moron stand on his head in the kitchen?
He was making an upside-down cake.

Did you hear about the moron who threw the clock out the window—because he wanted to see time fly?

Or the moron who shot the alarm clock because he felt like killing time?

There was a moron who wrote himself a letter and forgot to sign it.
When it arrived, he didn't know who it was from!

Did you hear about the moron who sprayed his apartment with DDT because he heard it might be bugged?

Did you hear about the moron who wore a wet shirt all day because the label said "Wash and wear"?

Why did the moron bring a ladder to his trial?
So he could take his case to a higher court.

Why did the moron jump out the window?
To try out his new spring suit!

Did you hear about the moron who buried his car battery because the mechanic told him it was dead?

Why did the moron feed money to his cow?
He wanted to get rich milk.

VERY LITTLE SENSE

Jim: "Did you hear about the race between the head of cabbage, the faucet, and the tomato?"

Jerry: "No, how did it end up?"

Jim: "The cabbage was ahead, the faucet was running, and the tomato was trying to ketchup."

Scoutmaster: "Let's get our bearings. You're facing north; west is on your left; and east is on your right. What's at your back?"

Scout: "My knapsack!"

Bill: "How can you get into a locked cemetery at night?"

Bob: "How?"

Bill: "Use a skeleton key."

He: "What kind of paper should I use when I make my kite?"

She: "I'd suggest flypaper."

Bill: "This match won't light."

Jim: "What's the matter with it?"

Bill: "I don't know. It worked all right a minute ago."

"I can tell you how much water runs over Niagara Falls to a quart."

"How much?" asked Jim.

"Two pints."

He: "What gadget do we use to look through a wall?"

She: "What?"

He: "A window."

Farmer: "This is a dogwood tree."
Tourist: "How can you tell?"
Farmer: "By its bark."

Him: "How did you find the weather when you were on vacation?"
Her: "Just went outside and there it was."

Driver: "I smashed my car up. I was out driving and I hit a cow."
Friend: "A Jersey cow?"
Driver: "I don't know. I didn't see the license plate."

Gentleman: "Doorman, call me a cab."
Doorman: "You're a cab."

The three-year-old boy was watching his six-year-old brother read a book. The little boy asked if he could really read. "Of course," said the six-year-old, without taking his eyes off the page.

"Then read something for me," said his brother. He pointed to the stove and said: "What does the writing on that stove say?"

"I just read books. I don't read stoves," said the six-year-old.

A woman called her friend at 4 A.M. and said: "I'm sorry to wake you at such an hour."

Her friend answered: "Oh, that's all right. I had to get up, anyway, to answer the phone."

Passenger: "When the train stops, will you please tell me at which end to get off?"

Conductor: "It doesn't matter, lady. Both ends stop."

He: "Have a peanut."

She: "No, thanks, they're fattening."

He: "Can you prove it?"

She: "Have you ever seen a skinny elephant?"

Mary: "What are you running for, Peter?"

Peter: "I'm trying to keep two boys from fighting."

Mary: "Goodness! What two boys?"

Peter: "Larry and me."

When they pulled the absent-minded professor, half-drowned, from the lake, he sputtered; "How exasperating! I've just remembered that I can swim."

Druggist: "Did you kill the moths with those mothballs I recommended?"

Customer: "No, I sat up all night throwing them at the moths, but I couldn't hit a single one."

Older Sister: "Why are you wearing my new raincoat?"

Younger Sister: "I didn't want your new dress to get wet."

Bill: "Did you know you can't send mail to Washington?"

Jill: "No, why not?"

Bill: "Because he's dead. But you can send mail to Lincoln."

Jill: "But he's dead, too."

Bill: "I know, but he left his Gettysburg Address."

Boy: "Why did Mickey Mouse go on a trip to outer space?"

Girl: "I don't know. Why?"

Boy: "Because he wanted to find Pluto."

"Can you stand on your head?"

"Nope. It's too high."

"That's a funny pair of socks you have on—one red and the other green."

"Yeah. And the funny thing about it is that I've got another pair at home exactly like this one."

Alice (answering the phone): "Hello."

Voice: "Hello, is Boo there?"

Alice: "Boo who?"

Voice: "Don't cry, little girl. I must have the wrong number."

Boy: "Did you hear about the rope joke?"

Girl: "No."

Boy: "Then just skip it."

Grow-Up: "Here, here! You mustn't pull the kitty's tail."

Little Boy: "Don't yell at me. Yell at the cat. I'm only holding. The cat's doing the pulling."

Pete: "What did one IBM card say to the other?"

Jill: "I don't know, what?"

Pete: "I'm holier than thou."

Father: "How many letters are there in the alphabet?"

Son: "I don't know."

Father: "You've been to school for four years and you don't know how many letters there are in the alphabet?"

Son: "Well, you've been to the post office and you don't know how many letters are there!"

Amy: "Did you know how many sheep it takes to make one sweater?"

Betsy: "No. I didn't even know they could knit."

First Cowboy: "Why are you wearing only one spur?"

Second Cowboy: "Well, I figure when one side of the horse starts running, the other side will, too."

"Lend me half a buck."

"I've got only forty cents."

"O.K. Lend me forty cents. You can owe me a dime."

"Good grief!" said the city slicker. "Why did they put the depot so far from the town?"

"I dunno," said the local yokel, "unless they wanted to get the depot just as close as possible to the railroad."

"I'm really in trouble!"

"What's wrong?"

"I've lost my glasses and I can't look for them until I've found them."

"I always make a game out of taking a bath."

"How interesting! What do you call it?"

"Ring around the bathtub."

He: "What do you get when you cross a movie with a swimming pool?"

She: "I don't know. What?"

He: "A dive-in theater."

A motorist was going down a one-way street the wrong way.

Policeman: "Do you know where you are going?"

Motorist: "Yes, but I must be late. Everyone else is coming back."

She: "I'm not myself tonight."

He: "Then we ought to have a good time."

"I heard something this morning that opened my eyes."

"Me, too—the alarm clock."

"I know only two tunes: One of them is *Yankee Doodle* and the other isn't."

Him: "Say something soft and sweet."

Her: "Marshmallow."

Jimmy: "The police are looking for a man with one eye called Stanley."

Larry: "What's the other eye called?"

Paul: "I can beat you in a race any day, if you let me choose the course and if you give me just a yard's head start."

Peter: "O.K., you're on. What's the course?"

Paul: "Up a ladder."

He: "How can you put yourself through a keyhole?"

She: "Tell me. How?"

He: "Write 'yourself' on a piece of paper and push it through a keyhole."

Harry: "My father is an Elk, a Lion and a Moose."

Larry: "How much does it cost to see him?"

Smart Jimmy took Stupid to the football game. Before the whistle blew, Smart Jimmy said, "I can tell you the score of the game before it starts."

"Yeah?" said Stupid. "Tell me."

"Why," said Smart Jimmy, "nothing to nothing."

Sally: "There was a girl in the butcher store who was five feet tall and wore size eight shoes. What did she weigh?"

Mary: "I have no idea."

Sally: "The meat."

"What are you doing?"

"Writing a letter to my little brother."

"You don't know how to write."

"That's O.K. My little brother doesn't know how to read."

Ted: "Do you know why Robin Hood robbed only the rich?"

Al: "No, why?"

Ted: "Because the poor didn't have anything."

A little girl opened the door of the new refrigerator and found a very small squirrel curled up comfortably on the lower shelf.

"What are you doing there?" asked the little girl.

"Isn't this refrigerator a Westinghouse?" asked the very small squirrel.

"Yes, it is."

"Well," said the very small squirrel, "I'm westing."

Fire Captain: "What's the only piece of fire apparatus that won't go up a one-way street?"

Rookie: "A fireboat."

Diane: "How was spaghetti invented?"

Ellen: "I have no idea."

Diane: "Some fellow used his noodle."

The rain came down in buckets, faster and faster, harder and harder.

"It's raining cats and dogs," sighed the girl.

"I know," said the boy. "I just stepped in a poodle."

Why did the little boy always stand on a ladder when he sang his song?
So he could reach the high notes.

Baby-Sitter: "Why did you put this frog in your sister's bed?"
Boy: "Because I couldn't find a mouse."

He: "Did you hear the joke about the boy who popped the cookie bag?"
She: "No."
He: "It's crumby."

"Do you have holes in your underwear?"
"Of course I don't have holes in my underwear!"
"Then how do you get your feet through?"

Him: "Do you mean to tell me you fell over fifty feet and didn't get a scratch?"
Her: "Sure! I was just trying to get to the back of the bus."

First Twin: "Wow, it's cold! My feet are frozen and they're sticking out of the covers!"
Second Twin: "Well, for goodness' sakes, pull them in."
First Twin: "Oh, no! I'm not putting those cold things in bed with me!"

Two ants were running like the wind across a cracker box.
"Say, for Pete's sake," puffed one of them at last, "what are we running so fast for?"
"Can't you read?" asked the other ant. "It says right here, 'Tear along the dotted line.'"

"Do you want to get next to something there's a lot of money in?"
"Sure."
"Well, go downtown and lean up against the bank."

ONE-LINERS

Take some friendly advice. Send your wits out to be sharpened.

Offer him a penny for his thoughts and you're being more than generous.

He's a second-story man. No one ever believes his first story.

— They call him "chocolate bar." He's half nuts.

The mold of which good skiers are cast is usually plaster of Paris.

A man bumped into an old friend in New Orleans and muttered, "How's bayou?"

A father spent a fortune sending his son to college and got only a quarterback.

Employees of a Boston candle factory have it pretty soft. They work only on wick ends.

Hurricanes are named after women because there is no such thing as a himicane.

The French horn player whose toupee fell in his instrument spent the whole evening blowing his top.

Behind every cloud there's a silver lining—hiding another cloud.

Rome wasn't built in a day, but it sure was polluted in a hurry.

I'm sorry I'm late, but it was raining and my sun dial wasn't working.

A girl I know is very superstitious. She won't work in any week with a Friday.

If at first you don't succeed, try, try again. Then quit. There's no use making a fool of yourself.

An empty purse is always the same because there is never any change in it.

One way to solve the traffic problem would be to keep all the cars that are not paid for off the streets.

The movie was a real sleeper. I slept through all ninety minutes.

Children are like flannel because they shrink from washing.

The world is getting to be such a dangerous place, a person is lucky to get out of it alive.

The two most beautiful words in the English language are: "Check enclosed."

The smallest body of water in the U.S. is Lake Inferior.

The ink drop was crying because his daddy was in the pen.

The Pope received the gift of an electric blanket which was called the Purple Papal Heater.

Mrs. Bigger had a baby who was bigger than she was, because he was a little Bigger.

A cannibal chief said a certain missionary shouldn't be boiled for dinner because he was a friar.

A violinist, when asked if it was difficult to string a violin, replied, "It takes guts."

Your sense of touch suffers when you are ill, because you don't feel well.

One good thing about being bald: It's very neat.

50

Insanity is hereditary; you can get it from your children.

We don't seem able to check crime, so why not legalize it and then tax it out of business.

She's afraid that if she leaves, she'll become the life of the party.

If cleaniness is next to godliness, how come Mr. Clean is not a religious object?

The difference between a book and a bore is: you can shut up a book.

Magic carpets from Arabia are powered by turban engines.

An astronomer was asked about flying saucers and replied, "No comet."

When a man marries, he gets sixteen wives: four richer, four poorer, four better, four worse.

WIT AROUND THE WORLD

Why were the Indians the first people in North America?
Because they had reservations.

What's the difference between the North and South Pole?
All the difference in the world.

What would you do if you found Chicago Ill?
Get a Baltimore M.D.

Why are telephone rates high in Iran?
Because everyone there speaks Persian to Persian.

What bus crossed the ocean?
Columbus.

What was the greatest engineering feat performed in the United States?
Wheeling, West Virginia.

Which people wear the biggest shoes?
The ones with the biggest feet.

If two California telegraph operators married each other, what would they become?
A Western Union.

As the waters of the Red Sea parted, Moses was heard to comment, "Why do I always have to go first?"

Why does the Statue of Liberty stand in New York Harbor?
Because it can't sit down.

Why is a canal a good place to keep money?
Because there are banks on both sides and locks every so often.

What people are the strongest?
Shoplifters.

What color is the North wind?
Blew.

What country are children happiest in?
Lapland.

What is the tallest building in the world?
The library, because it has the most stories.

Where were the first doughnuts fried?
In Greece.

Who invented gunpowder?
A woman who wanted cannons to look pretty.

A little girl had some blocks with letters on them. She was learning her ABCs with the use of those blocks, and one night before going to bed, she was playing with them. When she got into bed, she started to say her prayers, but she was so sleepy all she could say was, "Oh, Lord, I am too sleepy to say my prayers. Here are the blocks and the letters. You spell it out."

Jennifer was a little girl who told big lies. She received a dog for her birthday, but she told her friends she had received a tiger.
Her mother was very upset about her lying about the dog, and she said to her, "You go upstairs and tell God you are sorry about lying."
When Jennifer came down, her mother asked, "Did you tell God you were sorry?"
"Yes," Jennifer replied, "and God said that sometimes he finds it hard to tell my dog from a tiger, too."

There was an unusual auction at our church yesterday. All the parishioners were asked to bring something to auction off that they didn't have any use for—and forty women brought their husbands.

If the head of the United States is called the President, and the head of England is the Prime Minister, what is the head of Nova Scotia called?

The Bossa Nova.

"That means fight where I come from."

"Well, why don't you fight?"

"Because I ain't where I come from."

He: "What's the difference between a lemon and a head of cabbage?"

She: "I don't know."

He: "Boy, you'd be a fine one to send after lemons!"

Shipwrecked Gal: "Oh, oh! Cannibals!"

Shipwrecked Pal: "Come, now. Don't get into a stew."

Harry was walking down the street one day when he heard cries for help. A big man was beating a much smaller man.

"Here, you!" shouted Harry. "Leave him alone." And Harry jumped into the fight, and pasted the big fellow on the chin.

"Thanks," said the little man after he had pulled himself together. "That was very nice of you. Look here, we'll share this twenty bucks I took from him."

Ali Baba went up to the entrance of the cave and cried, "Open, Sesame!"

And a voice from the cave replied, "Sez who?"

A man approached another man and said, "I'll pay you one thousand dollars to kill my wife."

"A thousand dollars," the other man replied. "Why should you want me to do that? Think of all the years you have spent with your wife. Think of what that woman has given you all those years."

"You're right," the man answered. "I'll make it two thousand dollars."

"That new member of Student Council seems to have a pretty good opinion of himself," said the president.

"You're not fooling," agreed the secretary. "On his last birthday he sent his mother a letter of congratulations."

Snob: "My ancestors came over on the *Mayflower*."

Friend: "It's lucky for them. Immigration laws are stricter now."

Bobby: "Do you know that every time I breathe, a person dies?"

Larry: "Why don't you use a little mouthwash now and then?"

On a bus the other day a man got up and gave a seat to a woman. She fainted.
When she came to, she thanked him. Then the man fainted.

He: "What did the moon-boy say to the moon-girl?"
She: "How romantic! There's a beautiful full earth out tonight."

He: "Where did he meet her?"
She: "They met in a revolving door, and he's been going around with her ever since."

Fred: "He reminds me of Whistler's mother standing up."
Ted: "Why do you say that?"
Fred: "He's off his rocker!"

May: "Burt reminds me of a fence."
Al: "Why do you say that?"
May: "He runs around a lot, but never gets anywhere."

Boy: "Do you think Jerry's very smart?"
Girl: "Well, they say he has a photographic memory. The trouble is, nothing seems to develop."

"Say, mister, what time is it?"

"'Bout Tuesday, I'd say."

"No, what hour? I have to catch a train."

"Aw, Tuesday's close enough. There ain't no train 'til Saturday, anyhow."

Jack: "What's the difference between a tuna fish and a piano?"

Jill: "I don't know."

Jack: "You can't tune a fish."

Boy: "You dance very well."

Girl: "I wish I could say the same for you."

Boy: "You could if you were as big a liar as I am."

Joan: "Whenever I'm in the dumps, I get a new hat."

Susie: "Oh, so that's where you get them!"

A bank in New York was well known for its promotions where free gifts were given to new depositors.

A bank robber held up the bank twice, and during his second holdup a teller said to him, "Say, weren't you the robber who was here last week? Why are you back?"

"Well," the robber replied, "last week I didn't get my clock-radio."

Read in the will of a miserly millionaire: "...and to my dear brother, Stanley, whom I promised to remember in my will, 'Hi, there, Stanley.'"

Al: "People call him the wonder boy."

Mike: "They do?"

Al: "Yes, they look at him and wonder."

Little Cannibal: "Is that airplane good to eat?"

Mother Cannibal: "It's like a lobster, dear. You eat only what's inside."

She: "What are you, anyway, a man or a mouse?"

He: "A man. If I were a mouse, I would have you standing on the table and screaming."

"All this talk about back-seat drivers is bunk. I've driven a car for ten years and I've never had a word from behind."

"What sort of a car?"

"A hearse."

Victim (lying in the road): "What's the matter with you, are you blind?"

Driver: "What do you mean, blind? I hit you, didn't I?"

OCCUPATIONS

Circus Performer: "The circus hired me to put my head in the lion's mouth."

Jimmy: "Isn't that hard on the lion?"

Circus Performer: "Oh, no, his part of the act is a snap."

Customer: "I can't pay for this suit for three months."

Tailor: "That's all right."

Customer: "When will it be ready?"

Tailor: "In three months, sir."

"What happens to a ballplayer when his eyesight begins to fail?"

"They make an umpire out of him."

Boxer: "Isn't it a long distance from the dressing room to the ring?"

Opponent: "Yes, but you won't have to walk back."

First Man: "Larry is a very brave guy. I just heard he was the first person to skydive without a chute."

Second Man: "Where did you hear that?"

First Man: "At his funeral."

It was a jet flight to Paris. The stewardess became so upset with two loud children that she made them go outside and play.

What kind of raincoat does a doctor wear on a rainy day?
A wet one.

What is everyone doing at the same time?
Growing older.

Which American president wore the largest hat?
The one with the largest head.

What does a cowboy say at the end of a long ride?
"Whoa!"

Why are chefs so cruel?
Because they beat eggs and whip cream.

Who are the best letter writers?
Fishermen—they are always dropping a line.

Why is a cloud like a jockey?
They both hold the rains.

Why is a traffic policeman the strongest man in the world?
Because he can hold up a ten-ton truck with one hand.

Why do gardeners hate weeds?
Because if you give them an inch they'll take a yard.

What sort of offspring does a stupid florist have?
Blooming idiots.

If an athlete gets athlete's foot, what does an astronaut get?
Missile toe!

Why do boys and girls buy ice cream?
They can't get it for nothing.

Two bums were relaxing, doing absolutely nothing, just enjoying the warm sun.

"You know, I wouldn't trade places with a guy who had a million dollars," the first bum said.

"How about three million?" asked the other bum.

"Not even for three million," he replied.

"How about a guy who had five million?" the second bum asked.

"Not even for five million," he replied.

"Well, how about ten million?" the second bum asked again.

"Ten million. That's different," he said. "Now you're talking about real money."

Why did the bum climb the ladder to the roof?

He heard the meal was on the house!

Tramp: "Say, mister, can you give me two dollars for a cup of coffee?"

Mister: "Two dollars? A cup of coffee is never more than a quarter."

Tramp: "Oh, I know it. But I'm putting all my begs in one ask-it."

Housewife: "You should be ashamed to be seen begging at my house."

Tramp: "Oh, don't feel like that. I've seen worse houses than this one."

Question: Why is it dangerous to tell a secret on a farm?

Answer: Because the potatoes have eyes, the corn has ears, and the beans talk.

"I am most grateful," the speaker said to the man in the front row, "that you have remained here for my entire speech while all the others walked out."

"Don't thank me," the man replied, "I'm the next speaker."

City Person: "Mr. Farmer, why are you plowing your field with a steam roller?"

Farmer: "I'm raising mashed potatoes this year."

A man was waiting to make his speech and kept walking back and forth before he was to go to the rostrum.

"Are you very nervous?" someone asked him.

"Not at all," he replied.

"Then what are you doing here in the ladies room?"

Tramp: "Beg pardon, but do you happen to have some pie or cake that you could spare an unfortunate wanderer?"

Lady of the House: "No, I'm afraid not. Wouldn't some bread and butter do?"

Tramp: "As a general rule, it would, but you see, today's my birthday."

A speaker was having a difficult time with his audience, which kept heckling him. Finally, he couldn't stand it any longer, and he angrily shouted, "Wouldn't it be better to hear one fool at a time?"

"O.K.," a voice from the audience replied, "go ahead."

A woman came up to a speaker after he had just delivered his speech. "Did anyone ever tell you that you were a great speaker?" the woman asked.

"No," the speaker replied.

"Then, what made you think you were?"

"Can you oblige me with something to eat?" asked the hobo.

"Certainly," said the lady. "Go out to the woodshed and take a few chops."

A panhandler approached a man on the street and said, "Mister, could you spare three thousand, four hundred and sixty-two dollars for a new car?"

"Three thousand, four hundred and sixty-two dollars for a new car! That's some nerve!" the man replied.

"I know," the panhandler said. "That's what I said to the dealer when he told me the price."

Why did the dressmaker want to avoid the crowd?
She thought she would be hemmed in.

Policeman: "Miss, you were doing sixty miles an hour!"
She: "Oh, isn't that splendid! I only learned to drive yesterday."

Cop: "You were speeding."
You: "Sorry, Officer, but I didn't notice the speedometer. I was drinking at the time."

Judge: "I'll give you ten days or $50."
Prisoner: "I'll take the $50, judge."

Two tramps were going down the street on a hot Easter Sunday, grumbling.
"Who are they?" asked one man.
"Just a couple of hot cross bums," replied the other.

What letter does the shoemaker use?
The last.

What did the painter say to the wall?
"One more crack like that, and I'll plaster you."

What is a man called who steals ham?
A hamburglar.

Editor: "Did you write this poem yourself?"

Poet: "Every line of it."

Editor: "Then I'm very pleased to meet you, Edgar Allan Poe. I thought you were dead."

Man: "Why does a golfer wear two pairs of pants?"

Boy: "I have no idea."

Man: "In case he makes a hole in one."

His father said to a young Boy Scout: "Well, son, did you do your good deed today?"

"I sure did. Four other Scouts and I helped an old lady across the street."

"It took five of you?"

"Yes. She didn't want to go."

During a football game, one of the players had a couple of fingers badly smashed. The team doctor rushed him off the field and examined and dressed the hand.

"Doctor," asked the player anxiously, "when my hand heals, will I be able to play the piano?"

"Certainly, you will," promised the doctor.

"You're a wonderful doctor," said the happy football player. "I could never play the piano before."

64

A minister had to call a minister friend far away. Picking up the telephone, he said to the operator, "I would like to place a long-distance call."

"Station-to-station?" asked the operator.

"No," said the minister, "parson-to-parson."

Judge: "I find the defendant innocent."

Accused: "Thank you, judge. Does that mean I can keep the money?"

Why should soldiers be rather tired on the first of April?

Because they've just had a March of thirty-one days.

Mother: "My daughter has arranged a little piece for the piano."

Neighbor: "Good! It's about time we had a little peace."

"Congratulate me! I won the election!"

"Honestly?"

"Why bring that up?"

Judge: "Have you ever been up before me?"

Prisoner: "I don't know. What time do you get up?"

BUSINESS BEFORE PLEASURE

Hotel Guest: "Does the water always come through the roof like this?"

Hotel Owner: "No, sir. Only when it rains."

"What did you do last summer?"

"I worked in Des Moines."

"Iron or coal?"

"Bus Driver, can you tell me—does this bus stop at the river?"

"If it doesn't, there'll be one terrific splash!"

Boy: "What did the adding machine say to the cashier?"

Girl: "I don't know. What?"

Boy: "'You can count on me.'"

He: "Why did Mr. Smith sleep under the oil tank last night?"

She: "Because he wanted to get up oily this morning."

"Why, look here," said the businessman who was in need of a boy, "aren't you the same boy who was in here a week ago?"

"Yes, sir," said the applicant.

"I thought so. And didn't I tell you then that I wanted an older boy?"

"Yes, sir. That's why I'm back. I'm older now."

"What's the idea of hiring that cross-eyed man as a store detective?"

"Well, look at him. Can you tell whom he is watching?"

A farmer had a son who went to New York and became a bootblack. Now the farmer makes hay while the son shines.

Landlady: "I'll give you three days in which to pay your rent."
Student: "O.K., I'll pick the Fourth of July, Christmas, and Easter."

One day the boss called Jenkins into the office. "Jenkins," he said, "I'm giving you a hundred-fifty-dollar-a-week raise. And, by the way, Jenkins, you're fired."
"Why did you just give me a raise and then fire me?"
"I just wanted you to see what a good job you're losing."

Wife: "Well, what happened when you asked your boss for a raise today?"
Husband: "Why, he was like a lamb."
Wife: "What did he say?"
Husband: "Baa!"

"I've told hundreds of people where to get off," bragged the small, shy man.
"I don't believe you," said his friend.
"It's true," the little man replied, "I'm an elevator operator."

Customer: "I don't like the looks of that codfish."
Grocer: "If you want looks, lady, why don't you buy a goldfish?"

"I've just been reading about a machine that does the work of ten men. It almost has brains."
"Not if it does all that work."

"Are you looking for work, my man?"
"Not necessarily—but I'd like a job."

Employer: "So you want a job. Do you ever tell lies?"
Office Boy: "No, sir, but I can learn."

Shopper: "What grade eggs do you have?"
Grocer: "First grade, second grade, and third grade."
Shopper: "Well, I want some that have graduated."

The man entered a store, bought a cigar, and then left. Minutes later he dashed back.
"That cigar," he shouted, "is terrible!"
"It's all very well for you to complain," said the storekeeper. "You've got only one. I've got hundreds of the smelly things."

Customer: "How much are your four-dollar shoes?"
Salesman: "Two dollars a foot."

First Floorwalker: "Poor old Perkins has completely lost his hearing. I'm afraid he'll lose his job."
Second Floorwalker: "Nonsense! He's going to be transferred to the Complaint Department."

COMPLAINT DEPT.

Boss: "Miss Smith, your typing is terrible, and you are incompetent and habitually late for work."

Secretary: "Does this mean that this isn't a good time to ask for a raise?"

Mr. Stanley was always on the golf course. Seven days a week he could be found playing his favorite eighteen-hole course.

A friend asked him, "Doesn't all that golf playing interfere with business?"

"Not at all," Stanley replied. "I never play at the office."

When is a department store like a boat?
When it has sales.

"I always do my hardest work before breakfast."
"What's that?"
"Getting up."

A woman went to a dance studio to see about lessons.

"How much do you charge?" the woman asked.

"We charge fifty dollars for the first month and twenty-five dollars for the second month," the instructor replied.

"That's fine," the woman said. "I'll come the second month."

Lady Customer: "Can this fur coat be worn in wet weather?"

Clerk: "Lady, did you ever see a mink carry an umbrella?"

SCHOOL DAYS

Mathematics Teacher: "Now, if I lay three eggs here and five eggs over there, how many eggs will I have?"

Pupil: "Well, to tell you the truth, I don't believe you can do it, sir."

The math teacher was in a good mood. Instead of settling right down to math, he decided to tell the class a couple of jokes. Everybody laughed—except one girl in the first row.

"What's the matter?" asked the math teacher. "Haven't you got a sense of humor?"

"I don't have to laugh," said the girl student. "I'm transferring to another school Friday."

Teacher: "Stevie, your essay on *Our House* is word for word the same as your sister's."

Stevie: "Sure, teacher—it's the same house."

Teacher: "What's cowhide used for?"

Pupil: "For keeping cows together."

Teacher: "What is the highest form of animal life?"

Pupil: "The giraffe."

Teacher: "Mary, how far away were you from the right answer to that test question?"

Mary: "Only two seats away, teacher."

Pupil: "What has 12 legs, a brown fuzzy body, and purple eyes?"

Teacher: "I don't know. What has?"

Pupil: "I don't know, either, but it certainly doesn't look nice on your neck."

Swimming Teacher: "Now, girls, swimming is the best exercise for keeping you slim and beautiful. It's really good for the figure."

Student: "Did you ever look at a duck?"

Teacher: "Where was the Declaration of Independence signed?"

Student: "At the bottom."

The teacher had been giving a very long lecture on animals. When she finished, she decided to ask a few questions.

"Bobby, tell me where elephants are found."

"Elephants," said Bobby, "are such darned big animals that they hardly ever get lost."

Gloria (saying her prayers): "Please God, make San Francisco the capital of New York."

Father: "Why, Gloria, what made you say that?"

Gloria: "Because I said so in my examination paper today, and I want it to be right."

A man who has never gone to school may steal from a freight car, but if he has a university education, he may steal the whole railroad.

Boy: "My little brother is only three, and he can spell his name backwards already!"

Girl: "That's amazing. What's his name?"

Boy: "Otto."

Teacher: "Name two pronouns."
Student: "Who, me?"

Student: "I don't think I quite deserve a zero on this paper."

Teacher: "Neither do I, but it's the lowest mark I can give."

The clerk at the bookstore said to the student who was having a hard time in every subject, "Here's a book that'll do half your work for you."

"Wonderful!" replied the eager student. "Give me two of them."

Professor: "Why are you so late?"
Student: "Class started before I got here."

"My father and I, together—we know everything in the world."

"Yeah? What's the square root of 144?"

"That's one my father knows."

"O.K. If you're so smart, what's six and four?"

"Eleven."

"Nah! Six and four's *ten!*"

"Couldn't be. *Five and five's* ten!"

Father: "Well, son, how are your marks?"

Son: "They're under water."

Father: "What do you mean, under water?"

Son: "Below C level."

She: "I was out of town when the class play was given. Did it have a happy ending?"

He: "Sure. Everybody was glad it ended."

Bobby: "I don't know how to answer this question."

Billy: "What does it say?"

Bobby: "It says, 'Who was your mother before she was married?' I didn't have any mother before she was married."

Billy: "So you're going to school now! What will you be when you graduate?"

Davie: "Old, I think."

Teacher to late pupil: "Why are you late?"

Pupil: "Well, I saw a sign down the street that said: SCHOOL AHEAD. GO SLOW!"

Two boys were walking past a sign in front of a school, and one said to the other: "Do you know what P.T.A. means?"

The other said, "I'm not sure, but I think it means Poor Tired Adults."

Teacher: "Steve, who was the smartest inventor of all time?"

Steve: "Thomas Edison. He invented the phonograph so people would stay up all night and use his electric-light bulbs."

A five-year-old boy was working with his crayons in kindergarten, and his teacher asked him what he was drawing.

"A picture of God," the little boy said.

"But Robert," the teacher replied, "nobody knows what God looks like."

"They will when I get through," Robert answered.

"Are you a good student?"

"Yes and no."

"What does that mean?"

"Yes, I am no good."

Mother: "How did you do in your English grammar examination, dear?"

Child: "Fine, Mom! I made only one mistake, and I seen it as soon as I done it."

Teacher: "Name five things that contain milk."

Pupil: "Ice cream, butter, cheese, and two cows."

He: "I think our school must be haunted."

She: "Where did you ever get that idea?"

He: "Well, I always hear people talking about the school spirit."

74

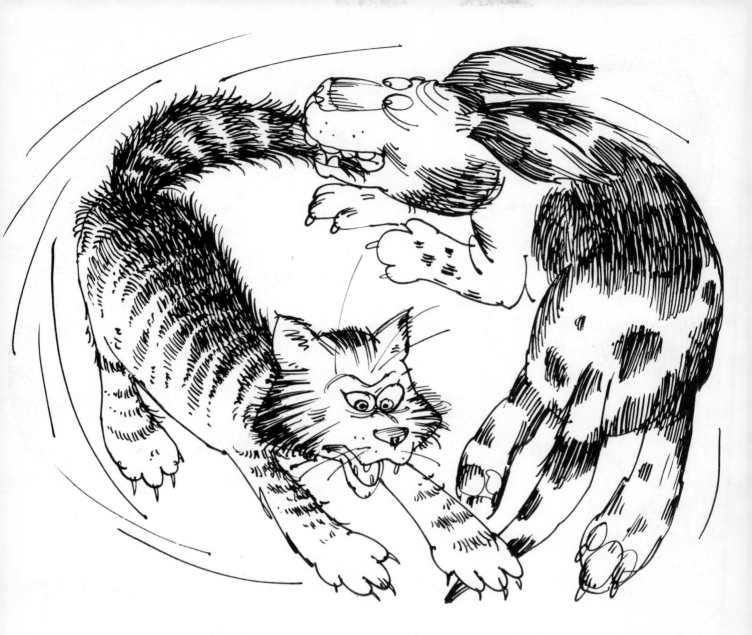

Teacher: "Susan, can you make up a sentence with the phrase 'bitter end' in it?"

Susan: "How about, 'Our dog chased our cat, and he bitter end.'"

Teacher: "Can you tell me anything about the great scientists of the eighteenth century?"

Student: "They're all dead."

The teacher called on Amy. "Tell me what you know about George Washington. Was he a soldier or a sailor?"

"I think he was a soldier," replied Amy.

"Why do you say that?"

"I saw a picture of him when he was crossing the Delaware, and any sailor knows enough not to stand up in a rowboat."

He: "What did the Pilgrims come over on?"

She: "The *Mayflower*."

He: "What did the midgets come over on?"

She: "Shrimp boats."

He: "And what did the doctors come over on?"

She: "Blood vessels."

Teacher: "You missed school yesterday, didn't you?"

Susie: "Not a bit."

In Sunday school, Jennifer, a seven-year-old girl, was telling her classmates the story of David and Goliath.

After Jennifer had finished, the teacher asked the class what that story taught them—and one little girl answered, "Duck!"

History Teacher: "In what battle did General Wolfe, hearing of victory, cry, 'I die happy'?"

Kid: "His last battle."

Teacher (to a boy trying out for a part in the school play): "Have you ever had any stage experience?"

Boy: "Well, I had my leg in a cast once."

Teacher: "Bobby, spell 'weather.'"

Bobby: "W-e-t-t-h-e-r."

Teacher: "Well, that's certainly the worst spell of weather we've had in a long time."

Teacher: "Give me, for any one year, the number of tons of coal shipped out of the United States."

Quiz Kid: "1492—none."

MOMS AND DADS

Fred's mother knit him three socks when he was in the army because Fred wrote he had grown another foot.

Mother: "If you wanted to go fishing, why didn't you come and ask me first?"

Jimmy: "Because I wanted to go fishing."

Dad: "I didn't sleep well last night."

Mom: "Why not?"

Dad: "Well, I plugged the electric blanket into the toaster by mistake, and I kept popping out of bed all night."

Paul: "Mom, we're going to play elephants at the zoo and we want you to help us."

Mom: "What on earth can I do?"

Paul: "You can be the lady who gives them peanuts."

Father: "Have you given the goldfish any water lately?"

Little Boy: "No, they haven't finished the water I gave them last month."

Mother: "Betsy, finish your alphabet soup."

Betsy: "No, thanks, mom—not another word."

Small Kid: "I wouldn't want you to say anything to my folks about it, but I don't think they know very much about bringing up children."

Baby-Sitter: "Where'd you get that idea?"

Small Kid: "Well, they make me go to bed when I'm wide awake, and they make me get up when I'm awfully sleepy."

Father: "My boy, I never kissed a girl until I met your mother. Will you be able to say the same thing to your son?"

Junior: "Yes, Dad. But not with such a straight face."

"It took me twenty minutes to write a message to the milkman," complained the wife.

"I watched you," said the husband. "Next time, why don't you write on the paper *before* you put it into the bottle?"

Robert: "Dad, gimme a dime."

Dad: "Robert, you're too old to be begging for dimes."

Robert: "O.K., Dad, gimme a dollar."

He: "All that I am I owe to my mother."

She: "Well, why don't you send her 30 cents and pay up the bill?"

A little boy who was seven years old had never uttered a word, and his parents were beginning to worry.

One evening at dinner, the boy turned to his father and said, "Pass the salt."

The astonished father turned to his son and said, "So you *can* talk! How come for seven years you've never said anything!"

"Well," the little boy replied, "up to now everything has been all right."

A little boy asked his mother, "Why can't we throw a dollar across the Potomac River the way George Washington did?"

And his wise mother replied, "Because money doesn't go as far as it used to."

Mother: "Billy, every time you play the violin the dog starts howling along. Can't you play some tune he doesn't know?"

Mother: "What did your father say when you told him you had smashed up the car?"

Son: "Shall I leave out the swear words?"

Mother: "Certainly."

Son: "He didn't say a word."

Small Daughter: "Why is daddy singing so much tonight?"

Mother: "He's trying to sing the baby to sleep before the baby-sitter gets here."

Small Daughter (thoughtfully): "You know, if I was the baby, I'd pretend I was asleep."

DINING OUT

"Do you serve crabs?"
"Sit right down, sir. We serve anybody."

He: "How much of that cheese did you eat?"
She: "The hole of it."

A man went into a seafood restaurant and asked for a plate of oysters. He started to eat them. Then he turned to the waiter and said, "These oysters haven't got any taste to them."
The waiter replied, "Wait till you strike a bad one."

He: "I see in the newspaper that a guy ate six dozen pancakes."
She: "How waffle!"

Customer: "I haven't come to any ham in this ham sandwich yet."
Waitress: "Try another bite."
Customer (after taking a large bite): "No, none yet."
Waitress: "You must have gone right past it."

Waiter: "Do you want the dollar steak or the dollar and a quarter steak, sir?"
Diner: "What's the difference?"
Waiter: "You get a sharp knife with the dollar and a quarter steak."

He was showing off in a restaurant. "Waiter," he ordered, "we want chicken—the younger the better."
"Yes, sir," replied the tired waiter. "Eggs."

Customer: "Is it customary to tip the waiter in this restaurant?"

Waiter: "Yes, sir."

Customer: "Then hand me a tip. I've already waited an hour for the steak I ordered."

Diner: "This lobster has only one claw."

Waiter: "I'm sorry, sir, the lobster got into a fight with another lobster and that's how he lost his claw."

Diner: "Then take him back and bring me the winner."

A condemned man who was to die at midnight was granted his last request, which was to be served an expensive French dinner by a typical French waiter. He also requested that the waiter not be told he was a condemned man.

The waiter arrived and served the prisoner in an indifferent and haughty manner. After the meal was finished, the prisoner turned to the waiter and said, "I'm sorry I don't have any money for a tip, but if you will come back tomorrow, I'll tip you then."

"Waiter, did I leave an umbrella here yesterday?"

"What kind of umbrella?"

"Oh, any kind. I'm not fussy."

Customer: "I ordered blueberry pie, waiter. This looks like pumpkin pie to me."

Waiter: "What does it taste like?"

Customer: "I don't really know."

Waiter: "If you can't tell the difference, it doesn't really matter, does it?"

"Waiter, this coffee tastes like tea."

"I'm sorry, sir. I must have given you the hot chocolate by mistake."

"Waiter, there's a fly in my soup."

"How much can a little fly drink?"

Waiter: "How did you find the meat, sir?"

Customer: "I just picked up the potato chip, and there it was."

"Waiter, what's this fly doing in my alphabet soup?

"Probably learning to read, sir."

"Waiter," said the irritated customer, "I don't like all these flies buzzing around my dinner."

"Yes, sir," said the eager waiter. "You just point out the ones you don't like and I'll chase them away."

"Waiter, this food isn't fit for a pig."
"Sorry, I'll bring you some that is."

"Waiter, this is awful—there's a fly in
my applesauce!"
"What did you expect, sir? It's a
fruit fly."

"Waiter, there's a dead fly in my
Jello."
"Sorry, sir. I'm sure he was alive
when he left the kitchen."

"Waiter, there's a fly in my chow
mein."
"That's nothing. Just wait till you
see what's in your fortune cookie,
sir."

Twas in a restaurant they met,
Romeo and Juliet.
He had no cash to pay the debt,
So Romeo'd what Juli-et.

Humpty Dumpty sat on a wall.
Humpty Dumpty had a great fall.
All the King's horses and all the
King's men
Came and ate scrambled eggs.

What did the tablecloth say to the
table?
"Don't move! I've got you covered!"

What do you get when you cross two
pizzas and handlebars?
A pie-cycle.

A lady was in a restaurant and said: "I want a cup of coffee without cream."

The waitress came back and said: "I am sorry, but we are all out of cream. Would you mind taking your coffee without milk?"

Written on a menu in a Texas restaurant: "Remember the á la mode!"

A typical waiter from a New York restaurant suddenly became very ill and was rushed to the emergency room of a hospital. He was lying on the operating table in extreme pain when he saw an intern walk by.

"Doctor, you must help me," the waiter pleaded.

"Sorry," the intern replied, "this isn't my table."

GOOD FOR WHAT AILS YOU

A frantic young mother called her doctor. "Doctor," the new mother sobbed, "my little baby just swallowed a bullet. What should I do?"

"The first thing," the doctor replied, "is to make sure you don't point him at anybody."

Doctor (on the telephone): "I'm sorry, but I can't make house calls at night."
Patient: "Next time I'll try to get sick before 6:00 P.M."

Cain was bad because Eve never read any books on child psychology.

Dentist: "I'm afraid it will cost you one hundred and fifty dollars to take out your wisdom tooth."
Patient: "Couldn't you take out a tooth with a little less education?"

A doctor spends four years in medical school and the rest of his life at the bank.

Doctor: "You're going to need a big operation if you want to live another thirty years."
Patient: "How much will it cost?"
Doctor: "Two thousand dollars."
Patient: "Couldn't I pay one thousand dollars for a smaller operation for fifteen more years?"

Patient: "Doctor, I'm worried about my diet. Do you think oysters are healthy?"

Doctor: "I've never heard one complain."

Patient: "Doctor, I've a pain in my left leg."

Doctor: "There's nothing I can give you for it. It's old age."

Patient: "But, doctor, the right leg is just as old as the left one and it doesn't hurt at all."

Patient: "I can't sleep these nights, doctor. I have terrible insomnia. What shall I do?"

Doctor: "Sleep near the edge of the bed. You'll probably drop off more easily."

Patient: "What shall I do? I have water on the knee."

Tired Doctor: "Wear pumps."

The doctor was very happy with his patient's progress. "You're coughing more easily this morning," he said.

To which his impatient patient replied. "Well, I ought to be. I've been practicing all night."

"Doctor, there's an invisible woman in your waiting room."

"Tell her I can't see her."

It was graduation time at medical school, and one by one the students visited the dean's office to say good-bye. The last student to visit the dean had the lowest grades in the class. "Peterson," the dean said, "your grades show a complete lack of understanding of medicine and a general absence of knowledge about the human body. It is our recommendation that you consider becoming a specialist."

A young man was very upset at having to pay doctor bills all the time. He bought a number of medical books. With the knowledge he gleaned from them, he became his own doctor for a year. But he eventually died of a misprint.

A distraught, disturbed woman rushed into a psychiatrist's office and shouted, "Doctor, Doctor, you must help me. I'm going crazy. I can't remember anything for more than ten seconds."
"How long has this been going on?" the psychiatrist asked.
"How long has *what* been going on?" the woman replied.

Why is a dentist unhappy at work? Because he looks down in the mouth.

"I always drink lots of milk, because my doctor says milk is a great bone-builder."

"Looks to me as though your drinks are going to your head."

Joan: "Susan, I heard your nephew drowned in a barrel of varnish. It must have been an awful way to go."

Susan: "No, he had a beautiful finish."

A young lady was visiting a man who was celebrating his ninety-ninth birthday. "I hope I'll be able to come and see you next year when you celebrate your hundredth birthday," the young lady said.

"Why not?" the old man replied. "You look healthy enough to me."

A patient was recovering from a serious illness in a hospital that seemingly specialized in bad food, rude nurses, miserable care. His doctor came to see him and said, "Mr. Lewis, I have bad news."

"What's the matter?" Lewis asked.

"Well, the tests show you have only a day to live."

"Oh, is that all?" he replied. "I was worried. For a moment I thought you were going to tell me I had to stay here another two weeks."

What's the best thing for hives?
Bees.

When is an operation funny?
When it leaves the patient in stitches.

First Patient: "Is your dentist careful?"

Second Patient: "Sure. He filled my teeth with great pains."

Man: "What's the quickest way to get to the hospital?"

Boy: "Just close your eyes and start across the street. You'll be there in a few minutes."

A lady went to a psychiatrist and said: "I'm worried about my husband. He blows square smoke rings."

The psychiatrist said: "This is an extremely clever feat. It must have taken considerable practice. But I don't see how it is a psychiatric problem."

"But doctor," she said, "my husband doesn't smoke!"

"My husband swallowed our alarm clock," the woman said as she entered the doctor's office.

"If *he* swallowed the clock, why did *you* come here?" asked the doctor.

"He bit me when I tried to wind it."

Boy: "Ugh! What's worse than finding a worm when you bite into an apple?"

Girl: "Finding *half* a worm."

Sure, an apple a day keeps the doctor away—but they never make house calls, anyway.

She got her good looks from her father—he's a plastic surgeon.

Nurse (on telephone): "Mr. Peters, you haven't paid your bill in two months, and the doctor is very upset."

Mr. Peters: "Well, tell him to take two aspirins and call me in a week if he isn't feeling better."

The psychiatrist asked the patient: "Do you have trouble making up your mind?"

The patient answered: "Well, yes...and no."

A woman ran into the doctor's office and said: "Doctor, I think I'm going crazy. I have a turnip growing out of my left ear."

"So you have," said the surprised doctor. "How can such a thing happen?"

"I can't understand it," said the amazed patient. "I planted radishes."

Patient: "This ointment makes my arm smart!"

Doctor: "Why not rub some on your head?"

The medicine-show man was bragging about his wonderful herb tonic.

"Yes, gentlemen," he said, "I have sold this tonic for more than twenty-five years and have never heard a word of complaint about it. Now, what does than mean?"

Smart Kid: "That dead men tell no tales."

Cat: "I'm not too well, Doctor. I keep thinking I'm a Great Dane."

Psychiatrist: "How long have you been feeling this way?"

Cat: "Ever since I was a puppy."

A well-known and highly successful doctor was rarely in his office. He was usually on the golf course. When a patient called on the phone, he would get a recorded voice saying, "The doctor is out. Please leave your message when you hear the beep."

Mr. Smith was getting fed up with the doctor's recorded messages; so he called, and when he heard the beep, he said, "This is the city morgue. Please tell the doctor three of his patients just arrived."

Anybody who goes to see a psychiatrist ought to have his head examined.

Saint Peter: "How'd you get up here?"
New Arrival: "Flu."

Who was the most successful doctor in the Bible?
Job, because he had the most patience.

Goliath was surprised when David hit him with a stone because such a thing never entered his head before.

A man walked into a psychiatrist's office loudly snapping his fingers.
"What are you snapping your fingers for?" the psychiatrist asked.
"To keep the lions away," the man replied.
"There aren't any lions around here," the psychiatrist replied.
"See?" the man said. "It worked already!"

A doctor called fat ladies who worry about their weight "hippochondriacs."

A doctor will always take care of poor people—even if it means making you one.

LIMERICKS

If there's one thing that Nature has
    taught us,
It's the virtues of being a tortoise.
    They can slumber, I hear,
    More than half of the year
In the depths of their snug winter
    quartoise.

A lady, while dining at Crewe,
Once found a dead mouse in her
    stew.
    Said the waiter, "Don't shout
    Or wave it about,
Or the rest will be wanting one,
    too."

You will find by the banks of the
    Nile
The haunts of the great crocodile.
    He will welcome you in
    With an innocent grin—
Which gives way to a satisfied smile.

There was a young lady named
    Bright
Whose speed was far faster than
    light.
    She set off one day
    In a relative way
And came back the previous night.

There was an old man from Nan-
    tucket
Who kept all his cash in a bucket.
    His daughter, named Nan,
    Ran away with a man,
And as for the bucket, Nan tuck it.

There was an old man of Tashkent
Who slept with twelve goats in a
    tent.
    When asked: "Do they smell?"
    He said: "Oh, yes, quite well...
But so far they don't mind my
    scent."

There was a young fellow of Wheel-
  ing
Who had such delicate feeling,
  When he read on the door,
  "Don't spit on the floor,"
He jumped up and spat on the ceil-
  ing.

There was a young lady from Niger
Who smiled as she rode on a tiger.
  They came back from the ride
  With the lady inside
And the smile on the face of the
  tiger.

A mouse in her room woke Miss
  Dowd,
She was frightened, it must be
  allowed.
  Soon a happy thought hit her.
  To scare off the critter,
She sat up in bed and meowed.

A cheerful old bear at the zoo
Could always find something to do.
  When it bored him, you know,
  To walk to and fro,
He changed it and walked fro and
  to.

For beauty I am not a star.
There are others more handsome, by
  far.
  But my face, I don't mind it,
  Because I'm behind it;
It's the problem in front that I jar.

There was a kind curate in Kew
Who kept a large cat in a pew:
   There he taught it each week
   A new letter of Greek—
But it never got further than Mu.

There was an old lady from Wooster
Who was often annoyed by a rooster.
   She cut off his head
   Until he was dead
And now he can't crow like he use-
   ter.

There was a young lady named
   Perkins
Who just simply doted on gherkins.
   In spite of advice,
   She ate so much spice
That she pickled her internal
   workin's.

A certain young fellow named
   Beebee
Wished to wed with a lady named
   Phoebe,
   But he said, "I must see
   What the minister's fee
Be before Phoebe be Phoebe
   Beebee."

There was a young lady of Lynn
Who was so excessively thin
   That when she essayed
   To drink lemonade,
She slipped through the straw and
   fell in.

RIDDLE ME THIS

Where did Abraham Lincoln go on his fourth birthday?
Into his fifth year.

Why will you never starve in the desert?
Because of the sandwiches there.

What's the best way to keep dried prunes?
Don't return them.

What color is a drop of water?
Pink, pink, pink!

When is your heart like a policeman?
When it keeps a regular beat.

Why should you never swim on an empty stomach?
It's easier to swim in water.

How many sides does a coconut have?
Two—inside and outside.

Why do Uncle Fred's slippers last so long?
He never wears them out.

What's always behind time?
The back of a clock.

Why is a clock like a condemned man?
Its hours are numbered.

What cane helps you move much
   faster?
A hurricane.

What never uses its teeth to eat?
A comb.

What is nearer to you than to me,
   but I can see it and you can't?
The back of your head.

What's the difference between· a
   watchmaker and a prison warden?
One sells watches and the other
   watches cells.

Where is generosity always to be
   found?
In the dictionary.

What bolt will you never find on a
   door?
A thunderbolt.

What makes more noise than a
   drum?
Two drums.

Which month has 28 days in it?
All months have.

What is it that you cannot hold ten
   minutes, although it is as light as
   a feather?
Your breath.

What pipes are never smoked?
Bagpipes.

What flower grows between your
     nose and your chin?
Tulips!

I have a head and a tail, but no
     body. What am I?
A nickel.

When your clock strikes thirteen,
     what time is it?
Time to have the clock fixed.

Four women were standing under
     an umbrella, but nobody got wet.
     How could this happen?
It wasn't raining.

Why do weeping willows weep?
They are sorry for the pine trees that
     pine.

What is never out of sight?
The letter "S."

What is never part of anything?
The whole.

What grows shorter as it lives
     longer?
A candle.

What did the jack say to the car?
Can I give you a lift?

What happens to little girls who eat bullets?
Their hair grows out in bangs.

What did the doughnut say to the rolls?
"If I had as much dough as you have, I sure wouldn't be hanging around this hole."

What's the difference between a high mountain and a spoonful of castor oil?
One is hard to get up and the other is hard to get down.

What did General Patton do with his boots when he wore them out?
He wore them home again.

What do you do with old bowling balls?
Give them to the elephants to shoot marbles.

What kind of song do you sing in a car?
A cartoon!

Why is thunder like an onion?
It comes peal on peal.

Who invented the steam engine?
Watts-his-name.

What's the price of the moon?
Four quarters.

How do you make a lemon drop?
Let it fall.

What scales can't be used for weighing?
The scales you play on the piano.

Why is the letter K a happy letter?
It's always in luck.

What flower is very fierce?
A tiger lily.

What tune makes everyone happy?
Fortune.

What has forks but never uses them to eat?
A river.

When was beef the highest it has ever been?
When the cow jumped over the moon.

If you throw a blue stone into the Red Sea, what will it become?
Wet.

What did the new suitcase say to the old one?
You're a sad case!

How would you clean your clothes if you were on a desert island?
Throw them in the ocean and let them be washed ashore.

What kind of robbery is not dangerous?
A safe robbery.

What is bought by the yard and worn by the feet?
A carpet.

What bell never rings?
A dumbbell.

What has two thumbs and no fingers?
A pair of mittens.

What did the tall chimney say to the short chimney?
"You're not big enough to smoke!"

What kind of berries live the longest?
Elderberries.

What did the mayonnaise say to the refrigerator?
"Close the door. I'm dressing."

What kind of a stone is a fake?
A shamrock.

How can you divide four apples among five people equally?
Make applesauce.

If you put a blue hat in pink lemonade, what will it be?
Wet.

What word has the most letters in it?
Mailbox.

What is the best month for a parade?
March.

Who was the most popular actor in the Bible?
Samson. He brought down the house.

What is it that you need most in the long run?
Your breath.

Why is a vacation in the mountains more expensive than one at the seashore?
Because everything is higher in the mountains.

What do you get when you cross a worm and a fur coat?
A caterpillar.

What does Santa Claus say when he works in his garden?
Hoe, hoe, hoe!

What stays hot in a refrigerator?
Mustard.

What falls often, but never gets hurt?
Rain.

What has two heads, six feet, one tail, and four ears?
A man on horseback.

What do you lose every time you stand up?
Your lap.

What is it that is alive and has only one foot?
A leg.

When do you have four hands?
When you double your fists.

Why does an Indian really wear feathers in his hair?
To keep his wigwam.

What goes farther, the slower it goes?
Money.

What is the best thing to take when you are run-down?
The number of the car that hit you.

What always has an eye open but can't see with it?
A needle.

What has a neck but no head?
A bottle.

What has eighteen legs and catches flies?
A baseball team.

What did Paul Revere really say when he finished his famous ride?
"Whoa!"

What causes a flood?
A river that gets too big for its bridges!

If your uncle's sister is not your aunt, what is she to you?
Your mother.

I can run, but I can't walk. What am I?
Water.

What do you do with a blue monster?
Cheer him up.

What's yellow and always points north?
A magnetic banana.

Why does a bald-headed man have no use for keys?
Because he has lost his locks.

What man shaves more than ten times daily?
The barber.

Life is tough...but what can you always count on?
Your fingers!

What became of that guy who stole the calendar?
He got twelve months.

What word is always pronounced wrong?

Wrong.

What is the quickest way to double your money?

Fold it.

What three-letter word is a mouse-trap?

Cat.

What ten-letter word starts with GAS?

AUTOMOBILE!

What question can never be answered by "Yes"?

"Are you asleep?"

What is the last thing you take off when you go to bed?

Your feet from the floor.

What is the difference between Donald Duck and an umbrella?

You can shut an umbrella up.

What is full of holes, but holds water?

A sponge.

Why does time fly so fast?
So many people are trying to kill it.

Where was the family when the fuse blew?
In the dark.

At what table do you never sit to eat?
The multiplication table.

What color is the newspaper when you have finished reading it?
Red.

If a biscuit is a soda cracker, what is an ice pick?
A water cracker.

What has many eyes and never cries?
A potato.

Why did the wagon train stop in the middle of the prairie?
It had Injun trouble.

Why did the baby strawberry cry?
Her mother was in a jam.

What did the rug say to the floor?
"Don't move, I have you covered."

What kind of shoes are made of
banana skins?
Slippers!

If two is company, and three is a
crowd, what are four and five?
Nine!

Why isn't your nose twelve inches
long?
Because if it were, it would be a foot.

Why is the lettuce the friendliest
vegetable?
It's all heart.

Where should a billsticker sleep?
In a fourposter.

Why is an old car like a baby?
Because it never goes anywhere
without a rattle.

What is green, lies in a ditch, and is
covered with cookie crumbs?
A Girl Scout who has fainted.

On what day should you eat the most?

Halloween—it's the best for a goblin.

Which moves faster, heat or cold?

Heat, because you can catch cold.

What time of the day was Adam created?

A little before Eve.

What did the big firecracker say to the little firecracker?

"My pop's bigger than your pop."

Which is the strongest day of the week?

Sunday, because all the rest are week days.

What is the difference between an old penny and a new nickel?

Four cents.

Why is an empty room like a room full of married people?

Because there isn't a single person in it.

What comes right up to the door but never enters the house?

The sidewalk.

Why is your nose in the middle of your face?

Because it's the scenter.

Question: Why couldn't anyone find the famous composer?
Answer: Because he was Haydn.

What has six feet and sings?
A trio.

What do a baseball team and a dish set have in common?
They both have pitchers.

When does it rain money?
Whenever there's some change in the weather.

Why is Sunday the strongest day?
Because all the others are weekdays.

What did one ear say to the other?
"I didn't know we lived on the same block."

Why is a crossword puzzle like a quarrel?
Because one word leads to another.

When does a boat show affection?
When it hugs the shore.

Question: What ring is best for a telephone?
Answer: Answer-ring.

Question: What day of the year is a command to go forward?
Answer: March 4th.

Why is S a scary letter?
Because it makes cream scream.

What always weighs the same, no matter how big it gets?
A hole.

Why didn't they play cards on Noah's ark?
Because Noah sat on the deck.

What did the toothbrush say to the toothpaste?
"I'm going to give you a squeeze when I meet you on the bridge."

What is the longest word in the English language?
Smiles, since there is a mile between its first and last letters.

Why do you salute a refrigerator?
Because it is General Electric.

What did one wall say to another?
"Meet you at the corner."

What did the ground say to the rain?
"If you keep this up, my name will be mud."

What is the difference between a hill and a pill?
A hill is hard to get up. A pill is hard to get down.

Four men fell in the water, but only one of them got his hair wet. Why?
Three of them were bald.